invite
PRESS

**Scan the QR code to visit
The Ping Life Facebook group**

The

PING
LIFE

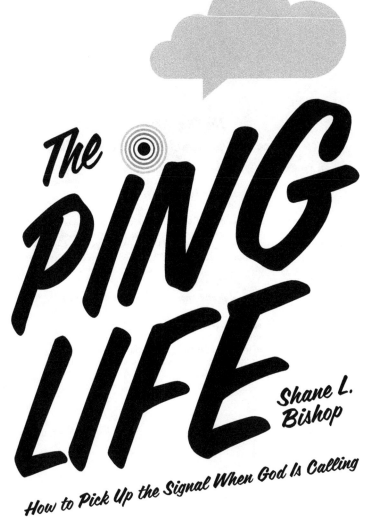

The PING LIFE

Shane L. Bishop

How to Pick Up the Signal When God Is Calling

invite PRESS

Plano, Texas

The Ping Life:
How to Pick Up the Signal When God Is Calling

Copyright 2023 by Shane L. Bishop

All rights reserved.

This book is printed on acid-free, elemental chlorine-free paper.

ISBN 978-1-953495-75-4; ePub 978-1-953495-76-1

Scripture quotations are taken from the *Holy Bible*, New Living Translation, copyright ©1996, 2004, 2015 by Tyndale House Foundation. Used by permission of Tyndale House Publishers, Carol Stream, Illinois 60188. All rights reserved.

23 24 25 26 27 28 29 —10 9 8 7 6 5 4 3 2 1

MANUFACTURED IN THE UNITED STATES OF AMERICA

Contents

Introduction: Ping!

Then I heard the Lord asking, "Whom should I send as a messenger to this people? Who will go for us?" I said, "Here I am. Send me."
—Isaiah 6:8

In the computer world, a *ping* is a transmission released by a network to see if a connected device may be reached. It is a signal in search of a response. In my world, a ping is a transmission released by God to see if a connected Christian may be reached. A ping is a heavenly signal in search of an earthly response. The *Ping Life* is a lifestyle of actively listening for God promptings, receiving them, discerning them, and actively responding to them. It involves keeping ourselves in the network with a personal commitment to be reachable by God. If you want an acronym, Power in Noticing God works just fine. The Ping Life is a path to soul fulfillment, Spirit-filled living, and ministry effectiveness. It is an exit ramp from constant guilt, stemming from the fact that we can't do everything, even with an exhausting works-based theology fueling the effort.

The Ping Life is a life of freedom.

The Ping Life is constructed upon a firm foundation of Christian discipleship. As serious followers of Jesus we should have well-developed prayer lives, participate in worship, spend time in God's Word, generously give of our tithes and offerings, find places to use our gifts in service, and offer an enthusiastic witness. In addition to these foundational disciplines, we should actively listen for God's promptings. When we receive a God ping, we should follow it up with decisive action.

Nothing more.

Nothing less.

Simple.

I remember receiving the ping to reopen live worship services at Christ Church during the early summer of 2020. The COVID pandemic had everyone shut down and weeks were turning into months. Nothing seemed to be improving. No other large churches in our region were open and the press seemed obsessed with reporting "superspreaders." It was quite easy to imagine a headline in a St. Louis newspaper or on the news entitled, "Illinois Mega-church Infects the Metro-East with COVID." Without a doubt, the easy thing to do was to go with the flow of staying closed. That decision would irritate a handful of folks, but the complaint box would remain relatively empty. Staying closed was the path of least resistance. Despite this reality, it was clear that God was asking me to reopen. Finally, the ping brought me to a crisis: I had to obey God or disobey. (I hate it when that happens!) I took my recommendation to our church board hoping to be overruled. They unanimously concurred. We were going to reopen.

As I pondered the potential ramifications of this move, it occurred to me that if we opened too early, half the country would criticize us. We would be utterly castigated in the press and lose much standing in the region. If we opened too late, the other half of the country would criticize us. We would lose massive credibility in hindsight. Then the life-shifting epiphany hit like a ton of bricks. It was my first true pastoral no-win scenario. No matter what we did, it was going to be wrong according to half the American population. We reopened. God protected us from the worst of COVID, the media circus never arrived, and in hindsight, it was one of the wisest moves we have ever made. We picked up hundreds of people because we had the courage to open! Hear and heed the pings, and every now and then, God will make you look like a genius!

The prophet Isaiah was pinged by God to a life of adventure. It is a reminder that God reserves the right to change the trajectory of our lives. The Ping Life is a world away from the rote, the predictable, and the mundane. We are secret agents for the Kingdom, embedded behind enemy lines and eagerly awaiting our next set of orders. Though we may look and feel entirely unremarkable, we are God's elite forces. Our mission is to live faithful Christian lives until God gives us a ping, and then we heed the ping whether it be large or small. We don't give orders; we take orders. We don't have the master plan; we are to fulfill our role in whatever God may be doing. We don't have to think; we simply have to obey. Ping heeded, we go on with our lives and await our next set of orders from God.

With discipleship baselines met, our spirits responsive to pings, and our hearts resolved to see pings through, we are freed to enjoy our lives, vocations, finances, friends, and families as blessings from God. The relentless, religious guilt that says we should always be doing more is removed! The Ping Life is:

- an exciting way to live as a faithful Christian;
- a sustainable way to live as a fulfilled human being;
- an exit ramp from a rote life of duty, guilt, and obligation;
- an earthly existence filled with peace, purpose, passion, and power!

And what's not to like about that?

Interested?

I thought you might be!

Chapter One

Freedom

Then Jesus said, "Come to me, all of you who are weary and carry heavy burdens, and I will give you rest. Take my yoke upon you. Let me teach you, because I am humble and gentle at heart, and you will find rest for your souls. For my yoke is easy to bear, and the burden I give you is light."
—Matthew 11:28-30

Not so long ago, I found myself forty pounds over my "fighting weight." Up to a few years back, I played a hundred softball games a year, worked out routinely to stay in shape, and ate like a teenager. Suddenly in my early sixties, I no longer played a hundred softball games a year (thus negating any need to work out) but still ate like a teenager.

They say your taste buds get more sophisticated as you age.

Didn't happen.

They say that your metabolism slows as you age.

Happened.

As time rolled on, I was getting increasingly . . . well . . . chunky. At first, I joked about my expanding horizons (I am a funny guy).

Then I got self-conscious, and then I tried to hide it. I don't know if you have ever tried to hide forty pounds but it wasn't easy. I bought bigger shirts, went up a size in pants, invested in a new belt collection, and avoided looking into mirrors of any kind. It all seemed good and well until I saw myself in a photo or a video. Horrible. Surely I didn't look like *that!* Then one day it all turned from self-deprecating humor into stone, cold condemnation. Condemnation is a terrible motivator. It shuts you down. I knew what I needed to do to take control of my health, I just couldn't find the will to do it. I don't know why launching into corrective action was so hard, but it seemed utterly impossible. I was in a decaying orbit, not just physically but emotionally as well. My spiritual life couldn't be far behind. Everything is connected. Something had to give.

Then God spoke to me. (Yes, I believe God speaks to people.) In the inner depths of my spirit, I heard God thunder, *It is true that you reap what you sow, but you don't reap today what you sow today. You reap today what you sowed yesterday, and you will reap tomorrow what you sow today. The good health you enjoy today is because you sowed good seeds yesterday. You kept yourself in great shape for decades, and you are reaping that good harvest. You are sowing bad seeds right now. Really bad. Unless you change course, your future harvest will not be to your liking.*

Terrible.

I like it so much better when God loves on me than when God shoves on me. Suddenly God had my attention.

Finally.

Then God sent a ping.

Not to me to minister to another person but to another person to minister to me. I hate it when that happens.

That person's name was Dan. Dan is a member of our Safety and Security team at church. He is sometimes assigned to follow me about on Sunday mornings as I meet and greet before, in between, and after our three worship services. (I have this image in my mind that every Sunday morning, the security detail draws straws, and whoever draws the short straw gets stuck with me.) One day, Dan sent a message to me: "Shane, I am a certified trainer. God has given me a ping to offer my services free to you. I was going to reach out a while ago, and I didn't follow through, but I am reaching out now. I can help if you seriously want to get healthier. I can keep you serving God longer. Let me know if you are interested."

It was the right message, delivered at the very moment I was most ready to receive it.

God is like that.

I was interested.

A couple of weeks later, Dan did an assessment and then designed a customized workout program for me. It was a routine I could complete at home rather than at a gym. That was perfect since my wife, Melissa, and I live in the proverbial middle of nowhere. The workouts would take a full hour, and I was to complete them three times a week. The program focused on flexibility, balance, and core strength. It was a workout for "go," not for "show." Dan constantly emphasized that creating and guarding three hours of workout time each week was both an investment in my future health and my future ministry. There were many times I wanted to skip a workout, but I knew how that story would end. Not only that, but how could I let Dan down, especially knowing he was helping me in response to a ping God had given him? I certainly didn't want my failure to follow through on my commitment to become a spiritual discouragement for him. I seemed trapped between a rock and a holy place. I had no choice but to get my physical life in order. I was in too deep. God gave Dan a ping. Dan gave me a game plan. It was time to run the offense. And I did.

I initiated the workouts. At first it felt awful, but in a few weeks it had improved from gut-wrenching agony to just all-out bad. Three months later, we rolled in the dreaded eating portion of the program. The strict diet would last for six weeks and essentially involved spitting out anything that tasted good. I had to change everything about the way I interacted with food, and instantly pivot from twenty-one splurge meals a week to none. Fast food breakfasts and tortellini lunches with ice cream chasers were out. More vegetables than I previously planned to eat in a hundred lifetimes were in.

There was no wiggle room.

No modifications.

No snacks.

It was a shock to my system. Almost immediately, the weight dropped off. I lost thirty-three pounds in six weeks. I kept losing weight after that. By the time things slowed down, I had lost forty pounds. After that, I was eased into an eating regimen that could occasionally include a pizza, an ice cream, or a Pop-Tart. Hopefully this new rhythm will propel me through my sixties. If it doesn't, I have eaten all kinds of yucky vegetables for nothing.

My problem?

The neglect of my health.

The catalyst?

A ping received and heeded by Dan.

My response to the offer?

"In!"

The goal?

A sustainable, healthy lifestyle.

The results?

So far, so good.

Sustainability will be the key moving forward. Weight is hard to lose, but it is *really* hard to keep off. I get it. There is a huge difference between eating a healthy meal and eating healthy.

Through the years, I have been asked to quantify a "sustainable" Christian life. People want a game plan! In response, I have developed a "baseline" for Christian discipleship. Surprisingly, my primary obstacle in developing this baseline was not the spiritually dry seasons; it was the highlight reel. Many of us have experienced incredible spiritual mountaintops throughout our lives, experiences like a life-changing pilgrimage to the Holy Land, a miraculous answer to prayer, leading someone to Christ, an unforgettable Holy Spirit moment, the salvation or baptism of a loved one, or an eye-opening mission trip. Experiences like these are as good as life gets in a fallen world.

These heightened spiritual experiences are terrific, but they are not sustainable.

They happen sometimes, but they don't happen all the time.

They are like places you go for a great vacation, but you can't afford to live there.

Let me tell you about two mission outreaches from my younger years that could not have possibly been more different or more the same.

San Pedro Sula, Honduras, Circa Mid-1980s

It had to be 106 degrees. You could cut the humidity with a knife. The second you emerged from the Grand Hotel Sula, your clothes were soaked. The acrid smell of street trash, raw sewage, and diesel fuel wafted in the hot, moist air. I was walking through a street market of sorts, an outdoor mall where business was conducted on the sidewalks. It stretched out for blocks and blocks. The dusty thoroughfare was lined with vendors on both sides, all actively staking their claim upon the streetscape as they competed for customers. This wasn't the kind of market that sold fruits or vegetables or the kind where tourists dicker with sellers over souvenirs made in China. This was a market that sold goods like pirated videos, knock-off sunglasses, cheap shoes, clothing proudly displaying high-end names, fake Rolexes, and various and sundry electronic devices. The children of the merchants played happily as we walked by; people were raising their families in these filthy streets. The more fastidious businesspeople attempted to sweep the dust off their space. One guy actually held a water hose to wash things down as his wife pushed the dirty water into the street with a broom. Vendors called out in broken English to those of us shuffling down the street, simply requesting we stop for a moment to examine their wares. It was a scene as old as civilization itself.

It was all more than I could take. I was emotionally overwhelmed. In that moment, I was immersed in urban poverty, Central American style, not the lazy or passive kind of poverty but the industrious kind. No one was looking for a handout. These people were working hard just to be poor, because it beat starving. They straddled an invisible line that had suddenly become most visible to me. A pessimism gripped me. The overwhelming majority of these industrious people would never get ahead, nor would their children. The world was stacked against them, and they didn't even know it. There were tens of thousands of them.

The discontinuity I felt as I put one foot in front of the other was palpable. It was an uneasy confluence of Christian compassion and first-world guilt. You couldn't caustically yell, "Get a job." These people had jobs but had little else.

I needed to do something.

I had to do something!

Then came the sobering epiphany that changed everything. If I completely liquidated my worldly assets, emptied my savings, and gave ten thousand of these people everything I had, these streets would look exactly the same tomorrow. I could never do enough to change the plight of these people. In fact, the combined resources of everyone I knew would not be enough to help these people. And even if it were enough to help here, I could find hundreds of cities just like San Pedro Sula all over the world. Not only that, no one seemed to be asking for my help anyway. They just wanted me to buy something. Not a one of them had a thing for sale that I needed or even wanted. "Give us this day, our daily bread." If that prayer was answered for them on this day, it came with no help from me.

Many years ago, I kept our checkbook on Quicken. At the end of every month when I entered the figures from our bank statement into the program, I would be between fifty and three hundred dollars off. Every month. The program would then prompt, "Do you wish to reconcile or adjust?" I always hit adjust. How does one "reconcile" what I experienced as a young man in San Pedro

Sula, Honduras? I don't think you do. You are going to have a find a way to "adjust."

Mardi Gras, New Orleans, Louisiana, Circa Mid-1980s

In 1986, I participated in a faith-sharing trip with "No Greater Love Ministries" to the New Orleans Mardi Gras. It was Fat Tuesday, February 11. The weather was cool on this particular morning, and the sun warmed things up as the day stretched on. The streets had taken a pounding from the partiers and smelled like vomit, urine, trash, and beer, mainly due to the vomit, urine, trash, and beer. A leftover person lay here and there, still passed out from the night before. They looked like human litter. You just stepped over them. As the day awakened and throngs of people pressed into the narrow streets of the French Quarter, I felt like we had taken a wrong turn on Canal Street and ended up in Sodom and Gomorrah. I had come to tell people about the Good News of Jesus, but no one seemed interested in Jesus at all. They came to get beads, get drunk, get loud, press beyond inhibition, and slake any fleshly thirst they might have. No one comes to the Mardi to get saved.

I found myself swept into the midst of hordes of people lining a highway to hell as though it were a parade route, but what could I do? Even if I led ten thousand people to Christ, it wouldn't make a dent in the depravity. I remember handing a bright orange Gospel tract to a guy about my age. It read "The Big Question" on the front and "If you died right now, do you have the assurance you would go to heaven" on the inside. He took the tract, glanced at the cover and dropped it to the ground. It all happened in less than a second. He didn't even look inside. I'm guessing he was not the inquisitive type. As I looked around, I noticed the street was literally lined with orange tracts. We gave them away and people threw them way. I was not going to lead ten thousand people to Christ, even if I spent every waking hour for the rest of my life attempting to do so. And even if I did, these streets would look exactly the same next year. Exactly.

How do you reconcile something like that? I don't think you do. You are going to have to a find a way to "adjust."

As different as they were, both of my mission trips impacted me significantly. I learned a lot about God, a lot about myself, and felt God's pleasure in my participation. I have no doubt that many of you can relate, but as you well know, there is an intentional and unmistakable downside. As a result of the spiritual mountaintops that we encounter 5 percent of the time, we can easily feel like we are not doing enough to serve God the other 95 percent of the time. This is the conundrum presented by works-based theology. You can never do enough. How can you help enough? How can you witness enough? How are you supposed to take your family camping in the Smoky Mountains when people in Honduras are being economically crushed and people at Mardi Gras are in danger of hell itself?

And then it starts.

The voice of the accuser. The one "who comes to steal, kill, and destroy": *How dare you enjoy your life?*

If you listen to that voice, things can quickly turn from a spiritual mountaintop into the "valley of the shadow" in about six seconds. Now that voice in your own head chimes in (as if Satan needs any help) to add to this cacophony of condemnation:

- I am not caring.
- I am not generous.
- I am not Spirit-filled.
- I am selfish.
- I am lazy.
- I am the lowest stave in the barrel of the Lord.

This is the whole problem, isn't it?

Many of us have experienced God undeniably use us for His glory, but like kids leaving church camp, we have to go back home, back to our marriages, back to our families, back to our churches, back to our jobs. It's as though the great butt of life sits on our spiritual whoopee cushion and forces all the Spirit-wind out. Once we are settled back in our routines, a haunting conundrum creeps in like a bitter aftertaste to what was a great cup of coffee.

How can we sleep at night, having seen what we have seen?

How can we go back to our ordinary lives, having experienced what we have experienced?

Is a sustainable Christian life even possible?

Is it wrong to be happy and enjoy life?

Is there a true path to freedom in Christ, or is the retail cost of discipleship a coin consisting of occasional passion and purpose on one side and lingering inner conflict and guilt on the other? My spirit has often screamed, *Jesus, "Is your yoke easy and your burden light" or is it not? Because I have to tell you, it isn't feeling very easy or light right now.*

Now for some good news.

I believe a joyful, purposeful, and sustainable life of exhilarating freedom in Christ is God's intention for us.

And all we need to get started is a baseline and a ping.

Chapter Two

Baseline

Once Jesus was in a certain place praying. As he finished, one of his disciples came to him and said, "Lord, teach us to pray, just as John taught his disciples."

—Luke 11:1

Jesus requires certain things from all of his followers. All of us. The word *disciple* derives from *discipline*. I call these things the Discipleship Baseline—disciplines and practices that are often crystalized in the membership standards and vows of many churches. After prospective members profess their faith and renew their baptism vows at Christ Church, they pledge to uphold the church with their "prayers, presence, gifts, service, and witness." Though this is not a book about establishing faith disciplines, I would argue that the Ping Life is built upon the foundation of Christian disciplines.

Let's develop that thought.

Prayer. We all know that we communicate with God through prayer, but we may forget that communication works both ways. For many, their prayer life seldom ventures beyond petition; it is a monologue rather than a conversation. Some see God as a DJ in the sky and prayer as a request line. The idea is to get God to do what you think God should be doing and if He does, you give Him praise or, perhaps, slip Him a $20. This misses the point of prayer. Prayers of petition are not intended to bend God to our will. They are intended to bend us to God's will. Petition is the upload, but we often forget that prayer is also God attempting to communicate with us. This is the download.

When I was a basketball coach at the grade school level, I taught the fundamentals of the game: dribble, defend, pass, rebound, and shoot. Among them was the necessity of finding a "passing lane" on offense. A passing lane simply ensures that the legal transfer of the basketball from one teammate to another is unobstructed by the defense before making the pass. Prayer is finding a passing lane with God, a path of unobstructed communication.

Worship. No act of personal piety or charitable enterprise can replace the central role of corporate worship in the life of a believer. Christians don't "have" to go to church; Christians "want" to go to church. Furthermore, Christians need not only attend church but make a true connection with God once they arrive. My wife, Melissa, defines the act of worship as the point "where our hearts and God's heart become one." The Greek word for worship, *proskuneo*, is a compound word combining the concepts of "turning toward" and "offering a kiss." In this sense, worship is an intimate act requiring our full attention. You can't worship *and* do something else; it is not a multitasking opportunity. If you are doing something else, you are not worshiping. If you are worshiping, you are not doing something else. Worship is not a weekly event we attend in a designated building for the purpose of navigating through an order of service. It is the air we breathe, the wine we drink, and the bread we eat. Worship is soul sustenance for the person of faith.

I am a sports fan, and among the things most fascinating to me is how some particularly rabid football fans approach live games. These games are not spectator sports for them; the fans are full-on participants! I have watched outdoor games being played in a blizzard and some fans have their shirts off, with their chests painted in team colors and a huge "D" in one hand and a piece of "fence" in the other. These are normally men wondering why they don't have dates, but I digress. Though I am sure they have consumed plenty of pregame "antifreeze," theirs is a commitment level that strikes me as impressive. To say these are "fair-weather" fans would be absurd. These guys are straight up in it! Not a one of them is checking their cell phone.

Now juxtapose these fans with the "it's too hot," "it's too cold," "it's too loud," "I can't hear" church crowd. Starting to get it? Worship is an "all in" enterprise! We need to approach worship with the enthusiasm, intentionality, and commitment of a football fan wearing a plastic cheese hat on a twelve-below-zero Sunday in Green Bay and leave our seat cushions, hand warmers, and lukewarm keg of weak sauce at home. Let's go big or go home.

Giving. The Old Testament establishes a tithe at 10 percent of our income. It is the literal meaning of the word. Nowhere in the Bible does it say not to tithe or that the tithe is abolished for Easter. The New Testament only adds that we should not use the tithe to excuse us from treating people well, and we should be in a good mood about giving. An offering is technically impossible until the tithe is fulfilled, as it is an "over and above" response to God's base-line. I tithe to the church and give offerings when and where God prompts me. We must also be willing to give all, should God ask. The tithe does not represent the bondage of legalism; it is quite the opposite. The tithe is freeing! After we give our tithes and offerings, what remains is a blessing from God.

When Melissa and I were first married, we were so poor we could only pay attention about four days a month. We wed between my junior and senior years of college and since I spent my final semester student teaching, there wasn't time for an additional job. She babysat for a working family and raked in $60 each and every week. I remember our discussion about tithing. I was wavering on the topic when she chimed in forcefully, "We are going to tithe $6 every week! We are going to give God something to bless." And we did. And God blessed us. I doubt our $6 a week impacted our church budget a bit but the choice to be faithful to God with our finances in those early years defined our lives and marriage.

Serving. Just because we can't do everything doesn't excuse us from doing something. The Bible teaches that the Holy Spirit has hardwired us with spiritual gifts that are to be used in the service of the Lord and within the context of the church. We each need to find a place (or places) to use our gifts, invest our time, and joyfully serve others in the name of Christ. Often, our place of service is found in direct response to what breaks our heart, what "turns our crank," or where God has previously moved in our lives. I often advise people looking for an entry point to service to ask themselves what they like best about our church and serve there.

Do you love our friendliness? Serve as a greeter, usher, or on the safety and security team! Do you love our children, special needs ministries, or student ministries? Plug in there. Do you love to worship? Join the worship team! Another approach is to assess your interests, training, and gifts and look for a good match when a need is presented.

There should be passion around serving! If you have three hours a week to volunteer for service, it should be the best and most rewarding three hours of your week! If where you are currently serving isn't working for you, exit responsibly and find a better fit! Serving allows God to flow through us toward others. Service consistently taps us into a life of purpose. We will not all be called to the same things or drawn to the same ministries but all Christians need to "find a place to serve!" Serving meets physical, emotional, and spiritual needs in the name of Jesus. It is rolling up our sleeves and getting our hands dirty. It can get messy but it will be God's kind of mess. Service is more than what we do as Christian people, it is who we are.

Witnessing. Evangelism is sharing the Good News of Jesus Christ under the influence of the Holy Spirit. To be effective, churches must make new Christians, turn them into disciples, and send them out to make new Christians. Churches must evangelize or they will die. It is that simple. The Great Commission of Matthew 28 is a clear directive from Jesus for his disciples to share the Gospel, and Pentecost gave us the firepower to accomplish the mission. Faith sharing is a mandate, but it does not have to be contrived or forced. We are not looking to shove square pegs into round holes, we are looking for square holes. These opportunities can come in the form of invitations to church, sharing a personal testimony, or praying on the spot with people in response to an articulated need. The only witness God can't use is a witness that is not offered. Our personal invitation or witness gives God something to bless!

Bible Study/Devotional Life. Many Christians today are functionally illiterate when it comes to the Bible. For years, I assumed a level of Biblical knowledge and understanding from my congregation that simply did not exist. Christians who do not know the Bible are prime candidates for heresy, spiritual manipulation, false teaching, and bad theology. God gave us but one volume. It consists of sixty-six books, compiles into two sections, and was written over hundreds of years. It is shorter than most James Michener novels. It is great to read Christian books and books based on the Bible or about the Bible, but that does not excuse us from reading the Bible. Being involved in intentional Bible reading plans and studies and small groups where the Bible is the "one and only" curriculum is an essential Christian discipline. Many Christians have only heard the greatest hits of the Bible. Careful study allows us to hear the whole album.

Fellowship. If salvation is received vertically (personal relationship with God made possible by the life, death, and resurrection of Jesus Christ), our Christian lives are lived out horizontally. Christians are "sticky." We are connected to each other. We need each other. The Jesus in us longs to connect with the Jesus in others. It is not lost on me that a characteristic of the early church was being in fellowship with one another. They didn't just go to church, they *did life* with each other. They shared meals, assisted each other financially, laughed together, cried together, and grew in faith together. My dad always defined *fellowship* as "a bunch of fellows on the same ship." That actually works. We need quality time with other believers. We need Christian friends. We need classes, small groups, book studies, and covenant groups. We need love and support. We need mentors, peers, and people to mentor. We need a place to belong that offers acceptance, challenge to be better, accountability, and support. Christians need a tribe. We need a community.

This discipleship baseline is not intended in any way to be exhaustive, only practical. The request of the disciples to be taught to pray was not solely a spiritual petition; it was a practical one. There are certain things that all Christians need to know how to do. This isn't about the electives; this is core curriculum. The basics. The baseline. When these faith practices are planted, rooted, functional, consistent, and operational, a firm foundation is built.

We are now ready to explore and embrace the Ping Life!

Chapter Three

Discernment

A ping is "a God-inspired prompting toward tangible action." Pings break static inertia and set objects at rest into motion. Every biblical call was a ping. Peter and John were going into the Temple and passed a lame beggar. Ping. Peter reached out his hand and commanded the man to walk. The man not only walked but went running and leaping with them into the Temple! Large or small, every person in the Bible who said yes to God responded to a ping! Pings communicate God's instructions for us, intentions to us, and aspirations for us. Pings take faith at rest and set it into motion. Pings connect us with a sense of divine power, passion, and purpose. Pings in accordance with scriptural teaching are how God leads us, grows us, speaks to us, and uses us to accomplish God's will.

Now let's address the elephant in the room.

How do you discern a God-inspired ping?

How do you know a ping is from God? How can you be sure that a ping received in the middle of the night came from God and not from those leftover wings (with ranch dressing) you ate at 1:47 a.m.? What if what you think is a ping is just a terrible idea and not from God at all? And what if the ping isn't small? What if it is HUGE? Shouldn't the discernment process be even more stringent then? These are fair questions to ask and can be illustrated by an account from the early days of my ministry.

God's Man of Power for the Hour, Fairview Heights, Illinois, Circa 1999

I believe it happened in the springtime, sometime after Christmas and before Easter. I don't remember the specifics of the *when,* but I will never forget the *what* of this story. I had been at Christ Church for almost two years, and my ministry was just starting to get some traction.

A sense that God may have something truly special for this congregation was just beginning to take shape in my heart.

In those days we had one worship service, and it started at 10:30. We were one church, in one location, who met at one time. Those were great days. I arrived about 9:30 through the front glass doors only to see a woman in a wheelchair out of the corner of my eye. I did not recognize her, so I said a quick "hello," and went to my office to get things ready for church.

When I emerged about thirty minutes later, she was in the same spot, so I went to introduce myself. A quick glance verified that she was not in the chair to convalesce but had been so confined for years and would be in that chair for the rest of her life. As I approached her, something welled up within me. Something in my spirit said, "Reach out your hand and command her to walk." I had read about a similar instance in the Bible concerning Peter and John and remember the encounter resulted in a once-lame man who went, "Running and jumping and praising God."

In a split second I was right in front of her. Would I obey God and set a miracle into motion, or would I miss God and make a scene that would embarrass the Lord (and His servant)? At the moment of truth, I held out my hand and said (drumroll please), "Glad you are here today." My goodness, I am friendly. Terrible. With that, God's man of power for the hour smiled, shook her hand, and walked into the sanctuary where I, no doubt, preached a stirring message about faith!

That scene haunts me to this day. It is the stuff of which opportunities are lost and bad dreams are made. What if I had really heard the voice of God in that moment? What if she would have reached for my hand, received divine healing, and went "running and leaping and praising God" throughout the narthex? How might that have impacted the church and my ministry moving forward? On the other hand, what if the ping wasn't from God at all, and I commanded her to "rise up" and nothing happened?

I will never know.

Thinking back, I believe that ping was most likely from God, and I was a leaf that fell from the lame tree. As the years have marched on, that scenario has never again presented itself in quite the same way. Perhaps I did the right thing. Missing God in that situation would have been catastrophic in every way. Perhaps I established that releasing such a huge ping toward me was a waste of God's time.

I will never know.

Looking back, I am convinced that I "ping-whiffed" that morning. God prompted me, fear fried the receptors of my discernment process, and I chose not to follow the ping with corresponding action.

I hate it when that happens.

Yet I determined something on that day that changed my life and ministry. That would never happen again. Moving forward, I would err on the side of obedience. If I felt the ping, I would go with it. Period. These days, I figure if I am going to strike out, I may as well go down swinging.

So, how is a ping discerned?

The Four Elements of a Ping

1. **Pings are initiated by God.** God has the master plan. God releases the signal. Our role is to respond. Pings move the Kingdom needle forward. Pings will never

contradict the clear and consistent teachings of the Bible.

2. **Pings prompt us to action.** God works through flawed people like you and me. Always has. Always will. A faith-filled response is always required on our part when we receive a ping. Pings are calls to action, not suggestions or public service announcements.

3. **Pings send us into crisis.** Never minimize the crises element that comes to us when God calls. Was that God or something else? Do we heed the ping or ignore it? The first crisis is one of discernment. The second is a crisis of obedience.

4. **Pings change everything.** Pings are catalysts. They are disruptive to the status quo. They are holy assaults upon the powers and principalities of this fallen world. They cut against the grain. Pings correctly heard and faithfully heeded are how God's will gets done in time and space.

Though we need to discern whether pings are from God, from our own imaginations, or from late-night tacos, we don't want to overthink them. My wife, Melissa, once told me, "If I followed through on one one-thousandth of my good intentions, I would be Mother Teresa." We get it, don't we? How many times have you talked yourself out of a God prompting by overthinking it? We take something easy and make it hard and then decide not to do the hard thing at all. I have long noted that Christians often don't think when we should, and we think when we should not. If temptation is coming your way, *that* is when you need to think. A great question to ask is, *Could anything good come from what I seem compelled to do?* If the answer is no, don't do it. Easy. Conversely, when pings come your way, you should ask, *Could anything bad come from what I seem compelled to do?* If the answer is no, I would err on the side of going with the pings. Finally, don't be fooled into thinking that missed pings only hurt you; missed pings hurt everyone. Christianity is not an individual sport; we are a part of a team.

I recall one ill-fated offensive play during high school football. I was lined up as wide receiver and went into motion. My job was to lead block on a sweep with the tailback following behind me. The coach told me to block the first guy I saw. Simple right? As it turned out, there were three defensemen headed directly toward our running back, and I couldn't block them all. I have no idea what or why I was thinking, but I let the first two defenders go and hit the third guy really hard. The problem was that the first two defenders tackled our running back for a sizable loss. Rather than do what I was told, I followed my own instincts and things went, well, poorly. I got yelled at after the play, and I got yelled at when we watched the game film the next morning. And I got yelled at the next week in practice. Nothing good happened there. My failure didn't just affect me. It had a negative impact on our entire team. In fact, right before my senior year concluded, our assistant football coach sent for me during study hall. I took the pass and went to the coach's office. I figured he was going to tell me that he loved me like a son or something. He looked at me, shook his head, and said, "Bishop, I have coached a lot of years and you are the worst blocking wide receiver I have ever coached."

That was it. I was free to go. We were both glad he got that off his mind.

If discerning pings seems daunting or is presently difficult for you, take heart in knowing that discernment gets easier as you lean into the Ping Life. Like everything else in life, we get better with practice, experience, and repetition. In the same sense a basketball player can hear a coach's familiar voice in a packed gym, or a lost child can hear her mother's voice in a crowded store, we develop an ear for the voice of Christ. After a while, the voice of Christ becomes unmistakable. Jesus said, "My sheep hear my voice, and they follow me." Also be encouraged in knowing that if you miss God on most pings, no harm was done. If you feel prompted to pay for the car behind you in the drive-through line and God wasn't really in it, it was still a nice thing to do. If that really wasn't a God prompting but you invited your new neighbor to church, it is still awesome and great good can come of it. On the other hand, you want to be REALLY sure it is God before you quit your job, sell all your earthly possessions, load up your family, and head for the mission field. All pings require discernment, but they do not all weigh the same.

Bible Pings

Pings are as fresh as a newly coined word and as old as God's initial attempt to speak to His creation. Let's explore the lives of a handful of Bible characters who heard the ping, heeded the ping, and changed the trajectory of salvation history. These are the heavyweights!

Abraham

And Abram believed the LORD,
and the LORD declared him righteous because of his faith.
—Genesis 15:6

Let's begin with the leading character of the Old Testament, the man who changed everything by responding to a single ping: Abram (a.k.a. Abraham). Though we have no real idea *when* Abraham lived, it was at least 3,500 years ago. We do, however, know *where* Abraham lived. Abraham's world was what we call the Fertile Crescent, the Cradle of Civilization. It was a harsh world that was surprisingly advanced, fallen, and depraved. We have no evidence that even one person living on the planet remembered, much less knew, the God of Creation. God was about to reintroduce Himself to humanity, and it came in the form of a ping. God found a unique man, made a unique promise, and established a unique people, from which would one day emerge a unique savior.

Our story comes from Genesis chapters eleven throught seventeen:

Abram married Sarai (say-rye) who was unable to have children.
It would appear that Abram's father, *Terah*, "wild goat," had made

something of himself in Ur because his children are given names of far greater stature. The name *Abram* means "exalted father," and the name *Sarai* means "princess" and implies noble birth. The two are half-siblings but, not uncharacteristically, marry each other in an attempt to keep the family wealth in the family. It was a better move for the bank account than for the gene pool. It appears this tribal group was enfranchised entrepreneurs. They no doubt had "Terah and Son" branded on their camels.

Terah took Abram, Sarai, and Lot and left Ur for the land of Canaan. But they stopped in Haran and settled there. There Terah died. Then the Lord told Abram, "Leave your father's house and go to the land that I will show you." God got Abram started in the right direction by pinging his father Terah to leave Ur. Upon hearing the Ping, an object at rest was set into motion. Terah is clearly a businessman of some sort with a case of wanderlust. The path forward was not a geometric move from east to west; that would take them across an inhospitable desert. They were much more traveling over a standing horseshoe, moving from the lower right side, up and over to the lower left side.

Though they started out for Canaan, roughly modern Israel, Terah settled in Haran (hay-run). Haran was a logical stop because it shared the religion of the moon god Nanna with Terah's native Ur. Since much ancient business was linked with pagan religion, Haran would have been a hospitable location for a Terah and Son franchise. Eventually, Terah died at the age of 205. It couldn't have been unexpected. At this strategic point, a God Abram does not yet know pings him to keep moving and to leave certain success for the unknown, and shockingly, he does just that.

The encounter between Abram and God happened solely at God's initiative, but why Abram? As you read the text, you get the inkling that God may have been waiting centuries for a man with the potential of Abram to emerge!

The potential for what?

The faith to hear and heed a ping! Next, God offers the most incredible promise in the Old Testament. It is the promise that changes everything:

I will cause you to become the father of a great nation. I will bless you and make you famous, and I will make you a blessing to others. I will bless those who bless you and curse those who curse you. All the families of the earth will be blessed through you. This is utterly staggering. This initial promise is a unilateral blessing with no human conditions to be met and no fine print! The promise includes legacy, fame, protection, and extended blessing. There has never been another promise quite like it.

The price tag?

Faith.

The retail cost of receiving God's promise was to believe it!

So, Abram departed and took his wife Sarai (say-rye), his nephew Lot, and all his wealth—his livestock, and all the people who had joined his household—and finally arrived in

Canaan. A ping heard became a ping heeded. Canaan became more than just a land; it became the Promised Land. The history of the Bible, from its earliest writings to the Jewish Revolt, to the Crusades, to today's world politics, has been a scrap over this piece of real estate. The House of Abram set out for the great unknown because an unknown God pinged and promised, and something in him dared to believe. Abram's emerging tribe then pushes south down the trade routes running parallel with the Mediterranean coastline. With each step (and even misstep) they get stronger and wealthier.

Then the Lord appeared to Abram and declared, "I am going to give this land to your offspring." And Abram built an altar in Shechem to commemorate the Lord's visit. God and Abram are getting to know each other. Shechem is about halfway between Galilee and Jerusalem, dead center of the Promised Land. Now God again speaks, "I will give you THIS land." With the promise now delivered and received, Abram faces the greatest challenge of all.

The waiting.

Then new challenges arise. Some Abram gets right. Some he does not.

Abram's Challenges

1. The Promised Land is inhabited, so until God is ready to bring Abram back to the Promised Land, his tribe pushes through and settles down in Egypt.

2. The House of Abram is a huge and wealthy people group that is seen as a threat to any region in which they settle.

3. Sarai is beautiful. Abram is convinced that the Egyptians will kill him to take her for their own, so he tells the locals that she is his sister. Sarai is taken up into the Pharaoh's harem but when God sends a plague upon the unsuspecting Pharaoh, he promptly returns Sarai to Abram and has them escorted from the country. So much for husband of the year.

4. The House of Abram is divided when Abram's nephew Lot falls into conflict with him. The source of the conflict? Water. Now each goes their separate way. One tribe has become two.

5. When a war breaks out in the region, Lot's entire household is taken as spoils of war along with the wealth of Sodom and Gomorrah. Abram converts his tribe into an army and rescues his nephew and many others as well.

6. Abram is blessed by the mysterious King of Salem and priest of God named Melchizedek. Apparently, someone *does* know God in this world after all. In response, Abram invents the tithe. He gives the priest a tenth of all the goods he had recovered rescuing Lot and returns the spoils of war to the plundered cities.

It had now been a long time since Abram received that initial promise from God. A long time. At times, it had to seem like a fading dream or a distant memory. Abram still believed God, but the game clock was definitely running.

The Lord spoke again to Abram, "Don't be afraid for I will protect you and reward you." But Abram replied, "O Sovereign Lord, what good are your blessings if I don't have an heir?" Abram calls God a new name, "Adonai Yahweh," which merges together the concepts of *master* on one hand and *covenant keeper* on the other. Abram is in full submission to God (master) and continues to believe the promise (covenant keeper) but is growing impatient. He then revealed to God the desire of his heart, a biological son to be his heir. It seemed clear that biology was not going to bring a child from his marriage, but Abram petitioned believing that God is not just a promise maker but a promise keeper. That being said, Abram and Sarai are *way* past child-bearing years, and no one else in the nursing home was really having lots of kids. God hurts for the hole in Abram's heart (as God had once hurt for the loneliness of Adam) and waxes poetically:

God said, "I will give you a son to inherit everything I am giving you. Look at the stars and count them if you can. Your descendants will be like that too many to count." Abram asks, "How can your promises come true when I don't even have a son?" and God responds, "I am the maker of sons!"

Abram asked for a single star, and God promised the Milky Way! God is like that!

And Abram believed the Lord and the Lord considered him righteous because of his faith. We often think of righteousness in terms of steady discipline, morality, and ethics, but Abram has not been particularly disciplined, moral, or ethical. What he does possess is an unshakable faith that the God who spoke to him in

Haran and made a promise in Shechem would do what He said. Abram has the ability to hear and heed a ping. To God, this kind of faith is worth all the righteousness in the world.

And they all lived happily ever after, right?

Not by a long shot.

Sarai had the horrible idea that Abram would sleep with her Egyptian servant, Hagar, and they would have a son by her. It was a ping-whiff of the first order. This arrangement produced a son, but rather than solve the problem, it complicated things even further. God will not be rushed. Sin brings complexity. Through no real fault of their own, Hagar and her son, Ishmael, are driven from the tribe. Abram looked at his biological son and said, "Good luck, kid." The clear intent seemed to be to let them die of thirst or starvation in the desert. From a human standpoint, the entire promise seemed offline due to human error. Abram was the human. If things were to move forward, Abram would have to up his game.

Then the Lord appeared to Abram and said, "I am God Almighty; serve me faithfully and live a blameless life." God just upped the price of the Promise. A unilateral promise has become a covenant. There are now conditions. It is no longer enough simply to believe in God. It is time to start displaying the character of God.

Abram fell with his face in the dust and God said, "I am changing your name from Abram (exalted father) to Abraham (father of many) for I will give you millions of descendants and kings

will be among them. This covenant will continue forever, and I will always be your God." Man down. Abram fell into the dust, and Abraham rose to his feet with a new covenant in his heart. Abraham lives in the blessing of God, is under an imperative to grow in the character of God, and his ear is ever more finely attuned to the pings of God.

The story of salvation history was launched when God decided to reintroduce Himself to a world who had forgotten her creator. God pinged a unique man named Abraham and made a covenant with him simply because he had the capacity to believe it and the will to obey. This interaction introduced a concept to the world we call faith. Faith is believing that God is who God is, and that God will do what God says, even if there is not yet evidence to support it. Such faith is essential to the Ping Life. The covenant centered upon the concepts of faithfulness on Abraham's part and blessings of life, health, and prosperity on God's part. From this gifted but flawed man, God forged a people group the Bible calls Hebrews, Children of Israel, Israelites, and eventually Jews.

Salvation history will not die on Abraham's watch.

Moses

*After this presentation to Israel's leaders, Moses and Aaron went and
spoke to Pharaoh. They told him, "This is what the LORD, the God of
Israel, says: Let my people go."*

—Exodus 5:1a

Abraham begat Isaac, Isaac begat Jacob.

God's tribe was settled in the southern regions of the Promised
Land when a famine buckled the knees of the ancient Middle
East. To save themselves from starvation, the descendants of Abra-
ham accepted an invitation to emigrate from Canaan to Egypt.
In the Bible, there is nothing wrong with Egypt (a lot happens in
Egypt) but it is not the land promised to Abraham. God blessed
His people in Egypt, but in time, they were systemically enslaved.
They were locked outside the Promised Land, as Adam and Eve
had once been locked outside the Garden of Eden. They had to
wonder if the Promise was forever offline. Let's face it, they had
abandoned the Promised Land. If the covenant was to get back
online, God would have to find a way to get them back to that
contested piece of real estate. Over the next four centuries, the
population of Egypt declined, and in accordance with God's

promise to Abraham, the population of the Israelites swelled. To build the great cities of Egypt, Abraham's descendants were transformed from herders to builders to slave labor, until systemic and oppressive slavery was all they could remember. When the people of God finally begin to cry out to God for deliverance, the story of Moses begins.

Moses was born an Israelite slave in Egypt. When the Pharaoh decreed that all Israelite baby boys were to be drowned in the Nile to control the slave population, Moses' mother set him afloat in the Nile. He was contained inside a basket made of reeds and placed where the noble women bathed among the bulrushes. He was discovered and adopted by an Egyptian princess and raised and educated in the palace. When the young man Moses saw an Egyptian unjustly beating an Israelite, he became consumed with anger and killed the taskmaster, hiding his body in the sand. The crime was discovered. Suddenly a fugitive, Moses fled to the remote deserts of Midian, married a shepherd girl, added value to her nomadic tribe, and raised a family. Whatever potential, promise, or sense of destiny Moses once possessed seemed forever gone. Because of one crime of passion (a ping-whiff of epic proportions), Moses had traded a prince's scepter for a shepherd's staff. He had gone from a nobody to a somebody to a nobody.

It all seemed over.

God wasn't even getting started.

Moses was keeping the flock of Jethro and came to Mt. Sinai. For forty years Moses watched another man's sheep and seemed content to live out his life as a common man. He had blown any chance at greatness and now dialed down his expectations to the extent that he could enjoy the simple pleasures of tending the flocks, living with the land, loving his wife, raising his children, being a part of a household, and getting to know the God of his ancestors. Moses had shown absolutely no ambition, and despite having a world-class education, he seems content to live out his life in obscurity.

Ping!

An angel appeared to Moses in the form of a bush, blazing but not consumed. Moses turned aside and when God called to him, Moses said, "Here I am." Much like the ping to Abraham, this prompting seemingly came out of nowhere. We tend to focus on the blazing bush, but the amazing thing here is that God reached out to a man who seemingly had no future. When Moses spotted the bush, the text says, he turned aside to investigate. When he turned away from his present reality and toward God's future, all kinds of odd things began to happen. First, he noticed that the bush was on fire, but the flame was not consuming the wood. Second, the bush spoke. That will throw you off. But the oddest thing of all is that Moses spoke back to the bush. In doing so, he uttered three words that would change the world, "Here I am."

Here I am,

- with a past but no future
- battered, broken, and flawed

- a common shepherd, in the middle of nowhere accomplishing nothing of significance
- a man with an education he does not use
- a leader who is leading nothing but sheep
- with nothing to offer

"Do you have business with me, God of Abraham? If you do, here I am."

Remove your sandals, you are on holy ground. Moses had to turn from the life he had to investigate whatever God might be trying to communicate. The text suggests that had he not turned toward the burning bush, the encounter would not have occurred. Perhaps he would have told everyone at supper, "Guess what I thought I saw today?" Turning *toward* a ping always requires turning *away* from something else. If we are to hear and heed the promptings of God, we will have to pause what we are currently doing. Once Moses turned, God spoke. Now, much like the conversation He once had with Abraham, God speaks yet again.

I have heard the cry of my people and am coming down to deliver them to a land flowing with milk and honey. Now go, I will send you to Pharaoh to bring my people out of Egypt. After four hundred years of slavery, God's people cried out to the God of Abraham, Isaac, and Jacob, and God heard their cries. God was going to take the descendants of Abraham from slavery in Egypt back to the land once promised to Abraham. Moses had to be hoping this was a PSA, but he knew better than that. Pings always ask something of us, and often it's what we least want to give. God's will is accomplished one ping at a time, in partnership with people like Abraham, Moses, you, and me. I have no doubt that if you said to Moses at that moment, "What is the last thing in the world you want to do?" he would have responded, "Go back to Egypt." At which God would have responded, "Perfect. Go back to Egypt." Moses now has a clear call to a very specific and unambiguous course of action. It is a point of crisis. He must now either heed the ping or walk away from it. It's that simple.

What does Moses do?

Like any sane person, he tries to get out of it.

Moses replied, "Who am I?" The only reason Moses was alive to begin with was that the Egyptians considered exile a greater punishment than death. When he fled Egypt, no one pursued him. He was disgraced. Moses had forfeited moral authority to lead anyone anywhere, and suddenly God wanted him to tell the most powerful man in his world to set the descendants of Abraham free. Why in the world would the Pharaoh do that? Why would the Egyptians let a legion of enslaved, semi-skilled laborers walk away during a building project? And for that matter, why would the Israelites follow Moses?

"Who am I?" was a good question.

I will be with you. When Moses asks, "Who am I?" God completely ignores him. It is as if God says, "Moses, this is not about YOU. This is about what I want to do, and I am offering you the opportunity to be a part of it! Let me tell you everything you need to know about this situation right now. If you heed my pinging, flaming bush-o-gram, I will be with you."

Pings always involve us but are never about us.

They are about what God wants to do.

Moses: "But suppose they do not believe me?"

God: "What is in your hand?"

Moses: "A shepherd's staff."

Moses still seems to be thinking this is about him. Here is the deal. He is the worst choice in the world. God pings him anyway. His staff represents the aggregate total of Moses' life to this point. The miracle that originally spared his life, his natural leadership, his world-class education, and his ability to act decisively, were all still there. Added to that was the character God had sculpted within Moses over the past forty years in the desert. Moses was now hardened by life and refined by fire. Moses was ready, but God knew it long before Moses did. God's message was clear, "Moses, I am the Creator of heaven and earth. I am not an idiot. If you didn't have what I was looking for, I wouldn't have pinged you."

God will never ping us to do what God has not equipped us to do.

God: "Now go!" (And stop getting on my last nerve!)

Moses: Please send someone else. God doesn't have to ping us to do things we were going to do anyway. God has never once pinged me to go to Buffalo Wild Wings and watch a St. Louis Cardinals baseball game, but God did have to ping me with a clear call to pastoral ministry. Like Abraham before him, God seems intent that Moses is His man and isn't likely to take no for an answer.

The Lord said, "Go to Egypt." And Moses went with the staff of God in his hand. Moses heeded the ping! And in good time, God used Moses to bring His people back to the very border of the Promised Land!

Challenging pings are often troubling. They shake us to our core and can have us wishing God would just let us be. Being a shepherd in Midian can't be all that bad. "Sheep smell and you get paid on Friday." Herding sheep in obscurity may seem like a uncomplicated approach to life, but that is not the pathway to a life of passion, purpose, and power.

Never has been.

Isn't now.

Isn't going to be.

Moses heard the ping.

Moses heeded the ping.

Salvation history was back online . . . again.

Chapter Six

Samuel

Meanwhile, the boy Samuel served the LORD by assisting Eli. Now in those days messages from the LORD were very rare, and visions were quite uncommon. One night Eli, who was almost blind by now, had gone to bed. The lamp of God had not yet gone out, and Samuel was sleeping in the Tabernacle near the Ark of God. Suddenly the LORD called out, "Samuel!" "Yes?" Samuel replied. "What is it?"

—1 Samuel 3:1-4

When it comes to Old Testament heroes, the odds always seem to be against them. When the chances are about zero, God is just getting started! Samuel is no exception. In fact, he had trouble just finding a way to enter this world. Samuel was born in the years before the formation of the nation of Israel, sometime in the late second century BC. His long life extended from the days of the Judges into the monarchy of Israel's first king, Saul. During this time, a formidable new enemy called the Philistines had emerged from the western seas. With their culture thriving, their five cities expanding, and their need for room expanding, they pushed into the inner mountain regions.

Israelite country.

God seemed silent, the priests were corrupt, and Israel was a loose federation of competing tribes. They were back in the right place but seemingly had everything else wrong.

Samuel's parents, Elkhanah and Hannah, were devout Jews who were served by two crooked priests, Hophni (Hof-nI) and Phinehas (Fin-E-us), the sons of the aged Priest Eli. Eli seemed to have been a good priest but a horrible father. Hophni and Phinehas are described as, "scoundrels with no respect for the Lord or their duties as priests." They did not respect God, stole from the men, seduced the women, and made mockery of God's Tabernacle.

It was a situation waiting to be rectified.

Hannah was loved by her husband, Elkhanah, but they could not produce a child. This reality broke her heart. As they worshiped at Shiloh, located in the low mountain ridge that runs through the middle of Israel, Hannah pleaded with God for a son. She vowed that if God gave her a son, she would return him to the service of God. Apparently, her prayer become quite frantic. After an embarrassing misunderstanding where Eli assumed Hannah to be intoxicated, he pronounced God's favor upon her, and she soon had a son named Samuel. True to her vow, when Samuel was weaned, she took him to Eli to be raised in the Tabernacle of God, where Samuel would become a priest. In the meantime, God had warned Eli to control his sons, but he would not, and their actions continued to damage the reputation of God. Time was running out on the priestly lineage of Eli. Israel would soon be in need of a true priest who could not only hear God but would obey God; a priest who would hear and heed a ping.

Enter Samuel.

Samuel was a Tabernacle kid, whose primary job was to assist and care for the feeble and almost blind Eli. Additionally, he pitched in to do anything that needed to be done. He reminds me of one of the cadre of "staff kids" who have grown up at Christ Church through the years. The Tabernacle was a semi-mobile, partitioned worship tent that would eventually become the immediate predecessor to Solomon's Temple in Jerusalem. Samuel lived in the Tabernacle with Eli, had a miniature priest's outfit, and slept near the Ark of God. You get the picture. One night when the boy was in bed, he heard a voice call his name: "Samuel."

Ping 1.

He rushed to Eli, who said he had not called and sent Samuel back to bed with a firm, "Beat it kid." But Samuel heard his name again.

Ping 2.

And again.

Ping 3.

The aged network finally recognized the signal and offered a response. Something in Eli remembered a time when God once spoke to humans, and he instructed Samuel to respond, "Yes Lord, your servant is listening."

Ping 4.

This time Samuel responded as Eli had instructed, and for the first time in a long time, God spoke to a human being, as humans speak to humans. Just as God had once spoken to Abraham and later to Moses, God told Samuel what God was preparing to do. It was a hard word for a loyal boy to hear and a heavy burden to carry. Eli's sons were evil, and in failing to control them, Eli had failed God. The House of Eli would soon be removed from the service of God and God's people.

Permanently.

Samuel was chosen to step into the vacuum.

What are you supposed to do with a message like that?

Samuel grew into a righteous man, God's favor was upon him, and everything he said was wise and helpful. The Bible reports that Samuel soon became a man to whom God spoke and through whom God spoke. In time, both his reputation and influence increased. When the Philistines attacked and defeated Israel, the warrior priest Samuel stepped into the leadership vacuum, picked up a sword, and united the descendants of Abraham. He drove out the Philistines, established peace, and began traveling town to town functioning as a judge, a general, and a priest. Samuel was a national figure. He was God's man, the undisputed moral leader of Israel, and everyone knew it. He was the universal joint linking the promise made to Abraham, to Israel's teetering theocracy, to Saul's monarchy.

In the Old Testament, men of moral courage and sterling and un-questioned character are hard to find, but Samuel is such a man. A man of courage and integrity. In its ethical sense, integrity points to core values, honesty, and a strong moral character that holds up under intense pressure. Samuel is not the most entertaining or flashiest character in the Bible. He has few unforgettable high-light reels, classic one-liners, or scandalous errors in judgment. If Samuel lived today, he wouldn't make the news all that much. But Samuel is the steel that supported the bridge that moved salvation history from Abraham to Moses, through the wild days of the Judges, and on to the kings.

Samuel was given to the service of the Lord as a child and never knew anything but the favor and presence of God. Samuel did not stray, he did not falter. Not only did he not break, he didn't bend. He learned to hear and heed God's ping as a boy, and as a man, the sound of God's voice became unmistakable to his ears. He led armies in times of war, established justice, upheld the law in times of peace, and was always the "strong right hand of God." No one in the Bible prevails quite like Samuel. He is a Biblical hero without the dark side of King Saul, the lapses in judgment of Gideon, the recklessness of Samson, or the complexity of David.

Samuel is not a king; Samuel is a maker of kings.

When I was a kid, people often gave testimonies in our small church in which they recounted their journeys of faith. I heard dozens of these growing up. I liked them. They generally followed this storyboard: "I was really, really bad; perhaps the worst person ever." And then they told their PG-13 rated "hippie" stories of sin, sex, drugs, rock and roll, heartbreak, and disappointment. That was the entertaining part. When they transitioned to, "Then I found Jesus," their lives seemed to get suddenly less entertaining. Samuel reminds us that the best testimony is often not having an entertaining part of your testimony to recount at all. "I loved Jesus from childhood, I grew up in the Lord, I am following Jesus as an adult, and God is presently using me in powerful ways," may be the best testimony ever.

One of the great gifts of my life was being raised in the Christian faith. Since my dad was a pastor, I did not have an idealized vision of the church. I knew it was a clay pot, but I have always believed in the love, forgiveness, and restoration offered by Jesus. I attended Sunday school, Wednesday nights, and Bible school; sat through worship; leaned into children's stories; and learned to pray, attend church, give, witness, and serve. Best of all, I was taught the word of God. I read the Bible from cover to cover in early high school, and by that time had memorized dozens of verses (in exchange for candy bars and other "exotic prizes"). I didn't always make perfect decisions, but I always knew that even when I got it wrong, Jesus could make it right. I was taught to hear God and obey God. This is why the Christian development of our children and grandchildren must be priority one! What is received when we are young becomes a part of us forever. Samuel learned to "hear and heed" the pings of God as a child and retained the practice throughout his life. He established that when you clearly recognize God's voice, obedience becomes much easier.

Samuel was more than a great man; he was a good man.

Salvation history barely survived the Judges.

We have Samuel to thank for that.

Chapter Seven

Nehemiah

They said to me, "Things are not going well for those who returned
to the province of Judah. They are in great trouble and disgrace.
The wall of Jerusalem has been torn down, and the gates have been
destroyed by fire." When I heard this, I sat down and wept. In fact,
for days I mourned, fasted, and prayed to the God of heaven.
—Nehemiah 1:3-4

Abraham received a promise, Moses moved God's people out of
slavery, and Samuel transitioned warring tribes into a nation, but
no one seemed to climb to the top of the hill in Canaan during
the Roaring BCs. At least not for very long. In 587 BC, Nebu-
chadnezzar II of Babylon (the Mesopotamian superpower of the
day) destroyed Jerusalem. It was a geopolitical and theological disaster. In addition to carrying the wealth of Jerusalem (and the
Temple) to Babylon, they stole the best minds of Israel in a classic
brain drain. These magistrates, intelligentsia, architects, members
of prominent families, artists, musicians, and skilled craftsmen
joined their blinded and shackled king Zedekiah on a thousand-
mile trek up and over a desert where they were assimilated into
Babylonian culture. Salvation history seemed in full retreat as they
literally retraced the journey of Abraham. When the Babylonians
fell to the Persians in 539 BC, the Jewish exiles found themselves

with a more sympathetic regime but still a long way from home, assuming they still considered Israel their home at all.

It is here that our story begins.

Nehemiah was a descendant of the Jewish exiles. He was also the chief administrator for the southern palace where the Persian king resided during the winter months. Official Title? Cup-bearer. It is 445 BC, and we are about halfway through the forty-one-year reign of Artaxerxes. Since poisoning was commonly used (in lieu of elections) to effect changes in national leadership, the cup-bearer would have ceremoniously tasted the king's wine and food before the monarch. Upon personal consumption, everyone would stare for a few minutes. If Nehemiah didn't begin to convulse and foam at the mouth, everyone could eat. Nehemiah would have been treated very well. Persian kings needed cup-bearers to be utterly convinced that their lives could not possibly be improved by the bribes of political opponents who wished to poison the king. Nehemiah would have been the highest-ranking government official of Jewish descent in Persia. He had done well. This account takes place in the southern capital city of Susa. Susa is one of the oldest cities in the world and is located in modern Iran. The ancient city would have been abuzz during the four months a year when the king and his court were in town.

The rest of the time?

It would have been hotter than six kinds of smoke in Susa.

Our story is launched by the visit of Hanani, a reliable source of information and possibly a blood relative of Nehemiah. People who were engaged in exotic or strategic travels would often be formally summoned by important people for vetting upon entering a city to make sure they were not spies. If they passed the interrogation, they went on tour. Seasoned travelers with gifts and "off-the-charts" communication skills were featured guests at banquets and royal interviews and spent much time publicly reporting the news of the world and telling stories of adventure.

Hanani received three questions from Nehemiah:

Question One: State of the People

I asked about the Jews who survived; those who had escaped the captivity. Most of the Jewish community after the fall of Jerusalem had not been exiled. Those who remained were primarily subsistence-level farmers or menial laborers who eked out livings around the charred rubble of the once-powerful city. These folks had more or less kept their racial identity for 140 years but had intermarried with the surrounding people groups, let faith lapse, and were poorly led. Due to a famine, the economy was now as broken as the city walls, and people were selling their children into slavery to surrounding people groups just to survive. The descendants of Abraham were consumed by hopelessness, faithlessness, and grinding poverty. Though Nehemiah was a Persian court official and would have lived in absolute opulence, his heart ached for Jerusalem.

Question Two: State of the City

And I asked about the condition of Jerusalem. The city walls lay in ruins. A city without walls was defenseless in antiquity, ergo, not a city at all. The "future and a hope" Jeremiah had prophesied so long ago for the exiles was first represented by Zerubbabel who led about fifty thousand Jews back with orders to rebuild the Temple. Zerubbabel was followed about sixty years later by the priest Ezra who reintroduced God's word to the inhabitants of Jerusalem. Much physical, spiritual, moral, and governmental progress should have been made by then. Nehemiah had hoped that these two leaders had done well in their work. They had not.

Question Three: State of the Wall

"The survivors are in great trouble and shame; the walls of Jerusalem are broken down and its gates have been destroyed by fire." Powerful and corrupt regional governors with much to lose had taken issue with the rebuilding of the temple and had convinced the king that the Jews were planning to rebuild and then revolt. Artaxerxes pulled his support and the suddenly empowered regional governors destroyed with prejudice what progress had been completed in Jerusalem to maintain their positions of power. So much hope had been placed in the reconstruction of Jerusalem and the restoration of God's promise to Abraham.

The comeback had been mounted.

The comeback had failed.

When I heard these words, I sat down and wept and mourned for days, fasted and prayed. Nehemiah's heart was heavy. His kinsmen were oppressed and news of the torn-down walls was devastating. The state of his people broke Nehemiah's heart. Was there something he could do for his people?

Ping!

Three months have now passed.

It is early spring.

Artaxerxes and his court were planning to leave the winter palace and travel north before the summer heat established its grip. If Nehemiah wanted to launch a formal request to the king concerning the state of Jerusalem, the request would have to be made in a rapidly shrinking window. In a culture where servants of the king were supposed to remain invisible and never call attention to themselves (Persian reliefs from the period sometimes show servants with their hands over their mouths, as not to offend the king), Nehemiah determined to take a big chance to heed his ping. When he stood before the king that day, he was not going to look or act like he normally did. If the king inquired, Nehemiah would take the risk that would either end his life or define it.

I had never been sad in his presence before. Things were heating up. When it was time for the pomp and circumstance of the ceremonial tasting of the king's wine, Nehemiah intentionally went before the king with something less than his "A" game. It was noted. This is the kind of ping about which you absolutely want to be sure or it will be the last ping you will ever have.

The king said, "Why are you sad (since you are not sick)? It must be a broken heart." Nehemiah replied, "How could I fail to be sad when the city of my ancestors lies in waste and ashes?" The ancient Persians placed great stock in their ancestors. That the city of a person's ancestors would be in ruins would be a great tragedy to the Persian mind. The king empathized, "Of course that would make you sad. That would make anyone sad."

"What do you request?"

"If it pleases you, send me to Judah to rebuild Jerusalem." Nehemiah requested that Artaxerxes overturn a direct order, give him an extended leave of absence, appoint him to the role of governor, and fully fund the project.

Hey, if you are going to ask . . .

There were plenty of reasons for Artaxerxes to deny Nehemiah's request. The king would lose a cabinet official, and since Nehemiah could not return by the next winter, he would have to entrust his life to a less trusted and less proven cup-bearer. The king would also have to authorize a shift in foreign policy that would create political unrest in Israel and perhaps even in Persia. But God moved upon the heart of the king, because there is always more going on with a ping than what appears to be going on. What was going on? Egypt at the far southwest corner of the Persian Empire was gaining strength, and a fortified Jerusalem would be of strategic importance as a physical buffer for a potential rebellion, an intelligence center, and a beacon to warn Persia of an invasion or revolt. Rebuilding Jerusalem suddenly made more sense than ever!

And the king granted his request.

Nehemiah was sent to Jerusalem to rebuild the broken walls, restore the broken people, and put salvation history back online. God pinged him to walk into an utter disaster where good leaders had failed before and present opposition was powerful and organized. Israel was in a bad place with few prospects, but help was on its way. God's help for the people of Israel was named Nehemiah, called by God, ready for the job, and prompted by a ping.

God's people had found their way back to Jerusalem . . . again.

Chapter Eight

Peter

A little farther up the shore Jesus saw Zebedee's sons, James and John, in a boat repairing their nets. He called them at once, and they also followed him, leaving their father, Zebedee, in the boat with the hired men.

—Mark 1:19-20

In this book, we have explored the lives of four very different leaders whom God pinged, and because they heard and heeded the ping, they changed the course of salvation history. Though Abraham, Moses, Samuel, and Nehemiah lived long ago, they are still impacting our lives today.

Now let's fast forward about five hundred years to the New Testament and explore the life of a man his mother called Simon and the Bible calls Peter.

A look at the life of Simon Peter takes us to the Galilee of northern Israel. We are in the third decade of the first century AD. Galilee is a name generally given to the region surrounding what we call the Sea of Galilee, then called Lake Tiberias. Yet this "sea" isn't a sea at all; it is a freshwater lake. Though its shores are sparsely populated now, the Jewish historian Josephus reported that the region had 204 villages and two major cities, Tiberias and Sepphoris. This region, featuring the breadbasket of the Valley of Jezreel, had changed hands often in ancient history. Tel Megiddo alone boasts the remains of twenty-six distinct civilizations. Few Jews remained in Galilee until a hundred and fifty years before Christ. The Jews that relocated there merged with many other cultures, religions, and people groups. By the time of Peter, Galilee was a confluence of ideas that represented a constant temptation to the monotheistic Jewish people. Jesus grew up about thirty miles west of the lake in Nazareth and later headquartered his ministry in a fishing village called Capernaum. The people who lived in this region were ethnically and culturally mixed, religiously eclectic, hard-working, hot-headed, and really didn't like the occupying Romans.

That is the setting.

Here is the story.

Mark 1: V. 14 Later on, John was arrested by Herod and Jesus went to Galilee to preach God's Good News. Jesus lived in relative obscurity for the first three decades of his life. But suddenly, the arrest of John the Baptist created a spiritual vacuum and Jesus stepped right in. John decreased, and Jesus increased. When John was executed by Herod Antipas, Jesus began to recruit and attract much of John's following and, more importantly, some of John's leadership base.

Enter Simon Peter.

V. 16 As Jesus was walking along the shores of Galilee, he saw two commercial fishermen: Simon (Peter) and his brother Andrew. Josephus tells us that in the time of Christ there were three hundred and thirty registered fishing boats working the waters of the Sea of Galilee, primarily fishing for a variety of tilapia we now call St. Peter's fish (I'll bet Peter didn't see that one coming). Fish were a staple in the diet of the Mediterranean world, especially for the locals. Unlike meat, fish were free and plentiful; you just had to catch them. The fishing industries also exported fish. Since they had no practical way to transport the fresh fish, the salt fish industry also boomed. Fish were caught by commercial fishermen, packed into salted barrels, transported to the Mediterranean Coast, loaded into cargo holds, and shipped all over the Roman Empire. This represents the physical, social, and economic world of Peter. He was a working man with a big personality, strong muscles, calloused hands, and he smelled like fish. He also had a capacity for God.

Peter was a natural Galilean leader—impulsive, boisterous, headstrong, courageous, opinionated—he led from the front. I picture him as a big and blustery guy with a thick shock of hair, a wild beard, calloused hands, a hearty laugh, and a rough exterior. He also possessed the inner capacity to become more than he or anyone else ever imagined. John the Baptist had grasped this capacity in Simon. Jesus recognized it as well.

V. 17 Jesus called to them, "Come and be my disciples and I will make you fishers of men."

Ping!

The offer was straightforward; leave your life behind and follow me.

No enticements.

No guarantees.

V. 18 *And they left their nets at once and followed him.*

Ping heeded.

Simon was originally from Bethsaida. He owned his own boat, was married (lucky girl), and he had a home in Capernaum. We also know Jesus changed his name from *Simon* to *Peter* (or *Cephas* in Aramaic), meaning "rock." As happened with Abram before him, sometimes the old name just doesn't fit the new man. Later, Jesus stated of Peter in pagan Caesarea Philippi, "Upon this rock I will build my church and the gates of hell will not prevail against it."

What kind of rock does Jesus need to build upon?

Most of us think this foundational "rock" needs to be level, consistent, immutable, and stable. It would be difficult to ascribe any of these virtues to Peter. When we think of ideal spiritual growth, we might think of a graph that moves "up and to the right" without setbacks, recessions, or adjustments. We receive Jesus, never miss another Sunday of church, read the Bible daily, and become paragons of holiness, goodness, and virtue. But for Peter, it didn't work that way. Peter's story is filled with peaks and valleys, chutes and ladders, triumphs and failures. No one got it more right or more wrong than Peter.

Let's probe a bit deeper into the life and times of Peter.

Matthew tells us that in the aftermath of the death of John the Baptist, Jesus had just healed the sick and fed five thousand men (not counting women and children). Miracles complete, Jesus instructed the disciples to transport him via fishing boat to the other side of the Sea of Galilee. Jesus had emptied himself. Then, he went into the hills to pray alone to be refilled. Time got away. Night fell and a storm blew in while the disciples were still waiting on the lake.

> *About three o'clock in the morning Jesus came toward them, walking on the water. When the disciples saw him walking on the water, they were terrified. In their fear, they cried out, "It's a ghost!" But Jesus spoke to them at once. "Don't be afraid," he said. "Take courage. I am here!" Then Peter called to him, "Lord, if it's really you, tell me to come to you, walking on the water." "Yes, come," Jesus said. So Peter went over the side of the boat and walked on the water toward Jesus. But when he saw the strong wind and the waves, he was terrified and began to sink. "Save me, Lord!" he shouted. Jesus immediately reached out and grabbed him. "You have so little faith," Jesus said. "Why did you doubt me?" When they climbed back into the boat, the wind stopped. Then the disciples worshiped him. "You really are the Son of God!" they exclaimed.*
> *—**Matthew 14:25-33***

This story describes a cycle that will continue to define Peter's life and ministry: awesome followed by terrible. Life for Peter is often a dunking booth. In three of the Gospels, Jesus asks the disciples who *people* say that he is. They offer an assortment of answers. Then Jesus asks who *the disciples* say he is. Peter replies, "You are the Messiah sent from God." At that moment, Peter is so ahead of the curve that Jesus tells him not to mention his epiphany to anyone. Peter is the first person who truly understands who Jesus is!

Awesome.

When Jesus begins to share with his disciples about his mission on earth - which would involve suffering, death, and resurrection - Peter, the team captain of the disciples, begins to sense morale waning. He rebukes Jesus, "Don't talk like that. You are freaking out all the kids." Jesus replies, "Get away from me, Satan."

Terrible.

Fast Forward to Holy Week. Jerusalem.

The Last Supper recounts those precious moments that Jesus spent with his disciples in an Upper Room in Jerusalem before all hell broke loose. The account is recorded in all four Gospels. When Jesus tells the disciples about his upcoming humiliation, suffering, and crucifixion, he prophesies that they would all abandon him. Peter swears he would not. "They might all abandon you Lord, but I won't." (That had to go over big with his teammates.) Jesus retorts, "Peter, you will deny me three times." In a rapid-fire sequence of events, Jesus is arrested on the Mount of Olives and undergoes a mockery of a hearing before the Jewish Council at the home of the High Priest. As Jesus had predicted earlier, all the disciples flee the scene . . . except Peter.

Give him that.

While people were waiting in the courtyard for the verdict, Peter is recognized by a young girl, who says, "This man is the leader of

Jesus's disciples." When he is asked, Peter denies Jesus and ironically swears to God that he doesn't know God's son. A rooster crows. Peter exits the courtyard in humiliation, fear, and disgrace; he weeps bitterly.

Jesus said, "The spirit is willing, but the flesh is weak." Indeed. Peter had failed once again, and yet when Jesus rose from the dead, Mary was given very specific instructions to tell "Peter and the disciples that Jesus had risen." Peter is still Jesus' guy.

Fast forward.

Jesus dies, is resurrected, appears to many, and ascends. Peter is filled with the Holy Spirit at Pentecost and becomes the top leader, preacher, and miracle worker in the early church.

And they all live happily ever after, right?

Wrong.

Years later, a Roman army officer named Cornelius in Caesarea has a vision in which God pings him to send for Peter, who at that time was staying in Joppa on the Mediterranean coast. To prepare Peter's heart, God reveals a vision in which Peter is commanded to eat nonkosher foods that lower from heaven on a blanket. Peter refuses, but God says to eat. The Big Idea: God does not show partiality.

With this, Peter goes to Caesarea and in so doing takes the Gospel message to the Gentiles. In time, Peter settles back in to lead the Jewish Christians and Paul emerges as God's unlikely instrument to the Gentiles. On this occasion, they are both in Antioch, probably the largest church of the mid-first century. Apparently, Peter was eating at the Gentiles' table before the Jewish Christians arrived, when for whatever reason, he disassociated from the Gentiles to sit with the Jews.

Paul called Peter out.

The Bible sided with Paul.

Peter being Peter was a party that never seemed to end. You could easily argue the man Jesus renamed "The Rock" never completely matured into a consistent and measured leader until much later in his life, yet we can point to many things about Peter we would do well to emulate:

Pinging Peter

1. **Peter believed first.** When no one got Jesus, Peter got Jesus. Peter was flawed in many ways, but he was also faith-filled and spiritually perceptive. He had a capacity for belief and an ear for pings!

2. **Peter stepped out of the boat.** Faith, rather than doubt, was Peter's first instinct. He was a ping heeder!

3. **Peter kept using his gifts.** Through all of the chutes and ladders that define Peter's life, he kept on listening, growing, and leading. Peter stayed at it and Peter got better!

4. **Peter never lost confidence God could work through him.** Peter was often wrong but never uncertain. He

believed Jesus could use a man like him for his glory. He was right.

5. **Peter was open about his miscues.** The denial story could have only come from Peter. The other disciples had run away. No one else was there. Peter is transparent, open, honest, and authentic. People can relate to that.

6. **Peter was the leader of the early church.** God doesn't work through perfect people because there aren't any perfect people. I am sure God would prefer to use straight boards with no knotholes, but in the absence of perfect lumber, God tends to use whatever He has! Peter was available.

7. **Peter truly lived.** Peter's life was filled with ups and downs but it was never boring.

8. **Peter was king of the comeback.** "The godly may trip seven times, but they will get up again." (Proverbs 24:16). Peter had both "foot in mouth disease" and the capacity to rebound from setbacks. Sometimes after taking an unexpected bath in the Sea of Galilee, you just have to dry off and determine to do better next time! Peter was often down but he didn't stay down.

You may be wondering how Peter died. Peter didn't die with Jesus during Holy Week, nor did he die of natural causes. Tradition tells us that upon his arrest and conviction during the terrorizing reign of the Roman Emperor Nero, Peter didn't feel worthy to be crucified like Jesus. At Peter's request, he was crucified upside-down in 64 AD.

How did Peter die?

He died well.

Salvation history has jumped from the Old Testament to the New Testament and will be entrusted to the church until Christ's return. This does not just refer to the early church. It includes the church of today. Us! If the prospect of the Church of Jesus Christ being entrusted to the likes of you and me makes you a bit nervous, it probably should. But keep in mind that we are not asked to develop the master plan; all we have to do is hear and heed the pings!

Chapter Nine

Salvation

Later on, after John was arrested, Jesus went into Galilee, where he preached God's Good News. "The time promised by God has come at last!" he announced. "The Kingdom of God is near! Repent of your sins and believe the Good News!"
—Mark 1:14-15

We have explored the lives of Abraham, Moses, Samuel, Nehemiah, and Peter. Finally, let's drill down into how the hearing and heeding of pings keeps moving the needle of salvation history. We might define salvation history as the jagged testimony of how God brought, and continues to bring, salvation to a fallen world.

The Bible opens in Genesis with God's creation of a breathtaking, primeval, and pristine earth. It was a complex world of brilliant design filled with beauty, innocence, and wonder. Everything about it was fueled by obedience to her creator. Humans were the crowning achievement of this world. We lived in union with God and were entrusted as stewards of all of creation.

The relationship between Creator and creation was built on a single concept: love.

Love was demonstrated by a single response: obedience.

Obedience and sublime perfection held for all of two chapters in Genesis but in the account of the Fall, Adam and Eve failed the conditions of love. God said, "don't," they "did," and a horrible virus called "sin" was unleashed upon the world. With sin came death. Humanity, once in perfect union with God, was now separated from God by willful disobedience. Humans were barred from the home God had created just for them, and the chasm separating Creator and creation seemed unfathomable. Had God simply walked away, it would have been perfectly understandable. We made this mess for ourselves. But God didn't step away, which is beyond comprehension. Love is relentless like that.

Not content with permanent estrangement, God decided to buy back what was already His. With this proclamation of intention, a cosmic war ensued for the future of humanity. God and Satan, good and evil, angels and demons, all took off the gloves. The battle was on. The Old Testament is the military history of that prolonged war. The final outcome was determined on Resurrection morning when Jesus of Nazareth rose from the grave; outcome—Christ's triumph over death. God's ultimate and final victory will be fully consummated when Christ returns. For now, we live in an "in-between" time when the outcome has been predetermined but the war is not yet over. Satan is going down, but not without a fight.

The Bible often illustrates itself with itself. For example, the Old Testament includes an R-rated story in the book of Hosea. You know the book is going to be dicey when it opens with God pinging the prophet Hosea, "Go and marry a prostitute so some of her children will be born to you from other men." I would have replied to God, "Hard pass." Surely that one had to be a late-night taco. Yet Hosea heeded the ping and married a prostitute named Gomer who would embarrass him, destroy his credibility, make him a laughingstock of the community, and never be faithful to him. Hosea would choose to love Gomer, and Gomer would break his heart repeatedly. Gomer's failure to faithfully love eventually landed her at the point of no return. She lost her freedom and was sold into slavery. Sin had made a captive of her, used her up, and spit her out. No one could have blamed Hosea for walking away, but he did not, which is beyond comprehension. Love is relentless like that.

Ping!

God pings Hosea in chapter three, "Go and get your wife again. And bring her back and love her." I would have replied, "Nope." Yet Hosea heeds the ping in verse two, "So I bought her back for fifteen pieces of silver, five bushels of barley and a measure of wine." Hosea *redeemed* Gomer. The cost of Gomer's redemption was negotiated in terms of silver, grain, and wine. The cost of our redemption was negotiated in terms of the blood of God made flesh. Hosea's pound of silver became Christ's pound of flesh.

Humanity was terminally and forever separated from God. The wound was self-inflicted. To get things moving in the right direction, God made a promise to a man named Abraham and built a people, delivered His people from Egyptian slavery through Moses, forged a nation under Samuel, mounted a comeback under Nehemiah, and offered prophecies of a messiah against all odds.

Then comes . . .

Nothing.

For four centuries between the Old and New Testaments, salvation history seemed to disappear like a river that suddenly plunges underground.

Out of sight.

Flatlined.

Then . . .

Seemingly out of nowhere, salvation has a heartbeat, found in the womb of a virgin. The conception of Jesus ushers in a new era in salvation history; the New Covenant has arrived. It took all of *that* to get to *this*. Jesus is conceived of the Holy Spirit and born of a common girl named Mary who lives in a small Galilean town. He is raised by a man named Joseph who, at the ping of God, marries Mary though she is carrying a child that is not his own. When a Roman census requires everyone to return to their ancestral home, Joseph and a very pregnant Mary make the eighty-mile trek south to the House of Bread, Bethlehem. There, Jesus is almost certainly born in a cave (though most of us visualize a barn) outside an inn, where animals are kept. When the brilliant, paranoid, and dying King Herod hears of a promised messiah being born in Bethlehem via the Magi, he orders the execution of every baby boy in the region.

Ping!

Joseph takes Mary and Jesus and flees to Egypt. Refugees.

Yes, Jesus lived in Africa. How did they finance the trip? Gold, frankincense, and myrrh.

Upon Herod's death and their subsequent return to Galilee, Joseph raises Mary's son as his own and teaches him a trade. Then the story of salvation history goes silent until Jesus is twelve and is taken to the Temple in Jerusalem. There he astonishes the priests and rabbis with his knowledge and insight. The kid has game. Things are going great, but . . .Mary and Joseph lose Jesus on the trip home.

Perfect.

Can you imagine the prayer? "God, about your son . . . he may or may not be lost." They track back to Jerusalem to find Jesus in the Temple. Jesus doesn't even know they are looking for him. "Didn't you know I would be in my father's house?" he says. Jesus obediently returns home to Nazareth, gets a good progress report, and we hear nothing more about him for seventeen years or so.

Then, a man called John the Baptizer emerges from the wilderness with animal skins on his back, locusts in his belly, fire in his eyes, revival in his soul, and water dripping from his hands. He is fearless and not on the payroll of anyone. No one has seen anything like him in centuries. It was like he made a wrong turn somewhere and ended up in the wrong testament. People are drawn to John from all over Israel, including his cousin, Jesus from Nazareth.

Ping!

Jesus is in motion. He follows the Jordan River south, attends a crusade, approaches John the Baptizer, and says, "Behold the son of God." Jesus is baptized in an act of radical identification with humanity. When he emerges from the water, the Holy Spirit comes down in the form of a dove, and God's voice is audibly heard, "You are my beloved Son, and I am pleased with you." Jesus is then driven by the Holy Spirit into the Judean wilderness in the Dead Sea region to be tempted by Satan. He passes the test. Now baptized in water, filled with the Spirit, and tried by fire, Jesus returns to Galilee.

Mark 1:14 reads, "Later on . . . John was arrested."

Ping!

Jesus immediately steps into the prophetic vacuum and begins to preach the Good News, "At last the time has come! The Kingdom of God is near! Turn from your sins and believe this Good News! Turn from your sins and believe in me!" It was almost as if he were reading one of John's sermons. We may well wonder, "*What* was this Good News?" but that is the wrong question. The proper question is, "*Who* is this Good News?"

JESUS WAS THE GOOD NEWS HE WAS PROCLAIMING!

Despite copious amounts of human mismanagement, salvation history had survived the Old Testament. The Old Covenant had been fulfilled and a New Covenant was in the making. A savior had been born. An infant had been protected. A boy had been raised. A young man had been equipped. A messianic ministry had been launched.

How?

One ping at a time.

Did You Hear Me?

"Anyone who listens to my teaching and follows it is wise, like a person who builds a house on solid rock. Though the rain comes in torrents and the floodwaters rise and the winds beat against that house, it won't collapse because it is built on bedrock. But anyone who hears my teaching and doesn't obey it is foolish, like a person who builds a house on sand. When the rains and floods come and the winds beat against that house, it will collapse with a mighty crash."
—Matthew 7:24-27

I wasn't worked very hard as a kid. Dad grew up on a farm, and I guess he figured he had worked hard enough for both of us. However, I was expected to hold up my end of the family arrangement. I was to keep my room spotlessly clean and my closet straight, make my bed each morning, and take out the trash. I didn't often get the opportunity to take out the trash because our small southern Illinois town allowed its residents to burn their own trash in backyard burn barrels, and Dad seldom missed an opportunity to play in a good fire. If you gave Dad some gasoline, a match, some flammable garbage, and a couple of aerosol cans, he could amuse himself for some time. Once he caught himself on fire, and I had to put him out. "Stop, drop, and roll" actually works, but I digress.

In addition to my chores, I was expected to do anything else Dad requested, and though he did not request often, he was most serious when he did. My normal approach was to ignore him when he gave me something to do, provided I was not in eyesight, and then hope he forgot that he needed me. Sometimes that worked, but when it didn't, and when I failed to get at the mandated task in a timely manner, he would lower his vocal register and sternly yell, "Son, did you hear me?" This was both a trick and a rhetorical question. To say "Yes I heard you" could be interpreted as an act of insolence (which was wholly unadvisable in dealing with my dad). There was a clear and direct connection between anything that could even remotely be construed as insolence and my life being made miserable. Conversely, to say that you didn't hear him demonstrated that your hearing was just fine.

I never responded.

It seemed the better play.

However, when I heard, "Son, did you hear me?" uttered for the third time with emotion and through clenched teeth, I would instantly drop what I was doing and engage my assigned task with feigned vigor. Thinking back, I was much better at hearing my father than obeying him.

Do we do the same with our heavenly Father?

Do we hear the pings of God?

And when we do, are we quick to obey? Or do we wait to be asked a few times, hoping God will forget?

In Matthew 7, Jesus combines his earthly and spiritual vocations. We know Jesus studied the law and knew God as his Father. We also know he was a carpenter and knew how to build practical and useful things out of wood or stone. (Mainly stone. Galilee wasn't exactly a forest). Jesus knew that to build a house in Galilee, you had to dig beneath the sand to carve your footers into the solid rock below. Jesus suggested in this teaching that all who hear his words are building a spirit-house. We might think of that house as our personal theology. Theology is not a big seminary word. It is the sum of what we believe to be true about God. All theologies look good during fine weather. Only when the storms blow do we see whether we have built something that will stand. Jesus teaches us that the destiny of the house built by the person who follows "hearing" with "action" is quite different from that of the person who simply hears.

In this parable, Jesus is not talking about the difference between believers and nonbelievers. He is talking about the difference between believers who hear and *do* and believers who hear and *don't* —ping heeders, as opposed to ping whiffers. Only when we choose to be both hearers *and* doers of the word does our spiritual house withstand the storms: our sails start to pop, our guilt is assuaged, and the adventure begins!

When Jesus pings, don't make him ask, "Did you hear me?"

And if you do, please don't make him ask three times.

Does heeding a God-ping to serve really matter? Really? I would guess only a tiny handful of the people who will read this book have heard of Junior Axley. Let me tell you how he has impacted your life.

Junior Axley was a volunteer youth director at the Sunfield Methodist Church in Sunfield, Illinois (a suburb of Du Quoin), over six decades ago. Junior was not a trained preacher, evangelist, writer, or theologian, but Junior Axley heard and heeded a ping. The ping was to serve as the volunteer youth director at a tiny community church and to mentor and love the young people entrusted to his ministry. Junior said yes to God, and in doing so, said yes to more than he could have imagined. One week, he led a fourteen-year-old farm boy named Freddie Bishop to Christ. He dared to suggest that there was more to the world than underground coal mines, Massy Ferguson tractors, and obligatory religion. There was a relationship with God possible through the life, death, and resurrection of Jesus Christ, and he simply invited Freddie into it. The invitation was accepted at the altar, where Freddie, my dad, prayed to receive Christ.

That simple response to Christ changed everything. Dad later received a call to ministry. After receiving his formal education and seminary training, he became a pastor at Oak Grove Baptist Church near Pinckneyville, Illinois, and served as a catalyst for the Jesus Movement in southern Illinois. After moving to San Antonio, Texas, to be a part of God's Love in Action (now Sammy Tippit Ministries), he was a part of a team that smuggled Bible and Christian materials into Communist bloc countries to equip the underground churches of the seventies. He founded his own ministry in 1975. Through No Greater Love Ministries, Fred Bishop has impacted the lives of tens of thousands of men. Through his evangelistic efforts, dozens of ministries have formed, thousands of disciples have been forged, and hundreds of thousands of people have found a saving relationship with Jesus Christ.

If my dad had not found Jesus, my life would have developed very differently, and though I don't know where I would be, I would not be here. If the ministries of Fred Bishop or Shane Bishop have touched you in any way (and if you are reading this book they have), Junior Axley has touched you as well. If Junior did nothing in his life other than heed a single ping and sow one gospel seed that bore one hundred-fold returns in Fred Bishop, he did something of Kingdom significance. After Junior relocated to be with Jesus, the spiritual interest from an investment in one teenager is still compounding at an unimaginable rate! You are now a part of that story and a part of that legacy.

Yes.

Heeding pings truly matters in ways you possibly can't imagine.

We may not all be a Fred Bishop, but we *can* all be a Junior Axley.

We can all hear and heed a ping.

Chapter Eleven

We'll Work Till Jesus Comes

So if the Son sets you free, you are truly free.
—John 8:36

Every now and then I hear the hymn, "We'll Work 'Till Jesus Comes." It was written by Elizabeth K. Mills and the lyrics dream of an eternal peace and rest *someday*, in the mist of the struggle and toil of *today*. It was included in over five hundred hymnals. Though the author was English, was born in the early 1800s, and only lived to be twenty-four years old, the song has endured. It further bears the distinction of being thoroughly "southernized, gospelized, and Americanized."

We hijacked it and flew it from London to Atlanta.

On my best days, the song is invigorating. The lyrics are sparse, the melody is simple, the harmonies are fun. It's everything that's great about a Southern gospel song! I have these nostalgic images of listening to the song on an AM radio while I sit under a shade tree on a blistering hot summer day, sipping sweet tea. On my worst days, the song is utterly exhausting. It is the emotional equivalent of sweating through your clothes on that same blistering hot summer day.

Will there be no rest until heaven?

There is so much to do and so little time! People are hapless and hopeless, lacking in even the most basic of needs. Others are lost in sin and in danger of hell itself.

How dare I rest!

I need to turn off the radio, put down my mason jar, get up, and "crack at it."

Arise ye slacker!

Then I remind myself to breathe. After creating the heavens and the earth, even God rested. God took a break, took time to enjoy creation, and perhaps went camping in the Smokies. The Ten Commandments prescribe a day of rest. It is essential to both Jewish and Christian traditions. The more I consider all of this, the more I enjoy the song. There is most certainly work to be done, but there is also the gift of life to be enjoyed. Finding balance is the key.

A handful of years back, Melissa and I checked out of suburbia. We sold our home located in a beautiful neighborhood into which we had sunk a lot of love (and a lot of money) and bought a cabin in rural, southwestern Illinois. The cabin is absolutely beautiful, sits in the middle of undulating wooded acreage, and is only visible by helicopter most of the year. It had sat empty for a couple of years, so upon purchase, we were faced with innumerable projects both large and small. Whether it was repairing the landscaping, staining and sealing the exterior, or cleaning, the work was often hard, but it was also a joy. This wasn't *a* cabin. This was *our* cabin. With a chainsaw, paint brush, shovel, or a rake in my hands, it felt like I was tending the Garden of Eden. It was not lost on me that working with our hands was something God gave humanity to do *before* the Fall! Work was on the list of items for consideration when God uttered his pronouncement, "This is good." Back before everything blew to crap.

Despite the enjoyable nature of the work, it still wore me out. Endless work is exhausting. It wasn't long until we noticed that we were spending every available hour working on the cabin but taking little time to enjoy the cabin. We had to remind ourselves that we didn't buy this property as a job. We bought the cabin to be our home! We couldn't just "work it," we needed to enjoy it! The tension between "doing" and "being" seemed particularly problematic since it was becoming clear that cabin life consists of endless and recurring projects (establishing why people live in houses and vacation in cabins).

We made an executive decision.

If we had two free days in a weekend, we would work one day and enjoy cabin living on the other. One day we were on the job. The next day we were on vacation. It was the secret sauce! With this simple declaration, we established a sustainable rhythm of hard and productive work and engaging in the simple task of enjoying our lives. We get a little "earth" most Fridays and a little "heaven" most Saturdays.

We have no way to right every wrong in the world, no way to assist everyone in need of help. We know that there is no way that we can personally share the Good News with everyone we see or lead everyone in the world to faith in Christ. Christian living isn't supposed to be a heavy burden we carry; instead, it is a beautiful and obedient life we embrace. If God pings you to participate in a mission trip, make a sacrificial financial donation to your church, volunteer for service, or lead a small group (and I hope God does), give it all you've got. Roll up your sleeves and enjoy your God-ordained workday. But when you get back home, take time to rest, replenish, and enjoy your life without guilt. Being a son, daughter, father, mother, brother, sister, coworker or friend is also God's work. So is enjoying a sunset, resting in a hammock, wading in a mountain stream, catching a fish, making good coffee, or watching a baseball game. These things are "good" as well.

Jesus came to set us free. He came to set us free from sin, free from a rote existence of duty, guilt, and obligation, and free from a grind-you-into-dust, works-based, theological construct. Salvation is not a prize to be earned, it is a gift to be received. We need to stop trying to earn from God the love He has already given to us freely. We can't right the wrongs of the Fall by our own efforts, but God didn't ask us to. That is what He asked Jesus to do. What we are asked to do is live obedient, beautiful, sustainable, and purposeful lives.

How Do We Live the Ping Life?

1. **Establish a discipleship baseline.** Hitting an occasional home run does not negate the imperative of practicing the fundamentals. Build a solid spiritual foundation.

2. **Listen for pings.** Radio signals are always in the air but we need a properly tuned radio to capture them. God is

always speaking. Our task is to make sure we are "dialed in" to God's calls to action.

3. **Learn to recognize God's voice.** When you are unsure, err on the side of obedience, especially concerning small matters where it can't hurt you or others, even if you have missed God's prompt. In time, God's voice becomes unmistakable.

4. **Heed the pings.** Decide to heed any and all promptings God may send your way. This keeps every ping from rising to crisis mode. You have predecided.

5. **Find a shady place to sit.** In the part of life that exists between the pings, remember that rest isn't just a recommendation, it is a theological mandate. We were not just created to "do." We were also created to "be." There is nothing wrong, and a lot right, with enjoying your life.

6. **Fill a mason jar with ice and strong, sweet tea, and sip it slowly.**

The Great Clipper Ping

In the late summer of 2022, Melissa was diagnosed with an aggressive form of breast cancer. It came out of nowhere. Within seconds of receiving the initial phone call informing her of the diagnosis, we were swept into a parallel universe. Many of you know this universe all too well. Chemo, surgery, and radiation over a period of months. There would be innumerable doctor's visits, tests, and waiting on the results of tests. The journey would be difficult and embarked upon without any guarantees. Melissa would lose her hair and her fingernails and toenails. She would suffer nausea, diarrhea, fatigue, and any number of equally unpleasant things. She would need emotional support and occasional help with medical care. Trying to get our heads around all of this was like drinking from a firehose. As we were still processing, it came. Wait for it . . .

Ping!

God spoke to my heart that my priority-one calling during this season was to be the best husband possible to His beloved daughter (and my beloved wife). This didn't mean I would take a Sabbatical; it meant that God was calling me to a singular and specific ministry. The ministry of a godly husband. I will never forget the day after a couple of chemo sessions when she asked me to cut her hair before it all fell out. We were in front of our detached log garage which sits uphill above our cabin, and I ran an extension cord out to power the clippers. She draped a towel around her shoulders, and I snapped on the #4 setting and carefully ran it through her hair. I followed with the #2 setting. Hunks had already fallen out. She said, "I am sorry you have to do this." I responded, "Caring for you is a joy." It was a pure joy. Serving Melissa in that moment was serving God. If I were feeding the ten thousand in Honduras or saving ten thousand at Mardi Gras, I would have been doing good but missing God. Ping-whiff squared. My theological task at that moment was to cut my Melissa's hair. As an added grace, despite my lack of aptitude, skills, or training, the haircut came out far better than it should have. She was beautiful!

Living the Ping Life isn't doing what you want to do or even what you think needs to be done. It is doing what God prompts you to do, when and where God prompts you to do it. In the Ping Life, there is no differentiation between the great and the small. There is only obedience and disobedience. We hear, discern, and heed; we leave the rest to God.

The Ping Life is not a burden; it is a joy.

The Ping Life is not a sacrifice; it is the path to freedom.

And while the Ping Life may not always be convenient or easy, it is sustainable.

And beautiful.

Welcome to *the Ping Life!*

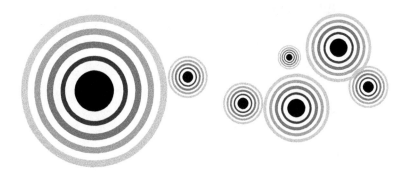

SCAN HERE to learn more about Invite Press, a premier publishing imprint created to invite people to a deeper faith and living relationship with Jesus Christ.

CPSIA information can be obtained
at www.ICGtesting.com
Printed in the USA
JSHW080941250723
45331JS00005B/10